Cwtch

Memories of a Life Loved in Wales

Marcie Layton

Huge Jam, 2021
First Edition

ISBN: 978-1-911249-68-9

Disclaimer: This book has been written from my heart. Where specific details have been forgotten, I have written in the spirit of the moment. Conversations, though recalled as accurately as possible, should not be regarded as verbatim transcripts. The names and identifying details of certain individuals and places have been changed to maintain anonymity. ML.

Dedication

This book is dedicated to Peter, my understanding husband, and our two fantastic boys. We have shared many happy times in our lovely little cottage. The privilege of knowing you is the biggest cwtch of all.

Special Thanks

I would like to thank the residents of Llangwm, for welcoming us into their community and into their lives. We may not actually be related to anyone in the village, but we feel connected nonetheless.

Thank you to the artist Cecilia Gatehouse (www.ceciliagatehouse.co.uk) for allowing me to use a photo of her wonderful wire drawing "Outing I" as the cover image for this book.

I would also like to thank my long-time friend Susan, for her support, and her humour, while I made the transition from city to country.

This book would not have been possible without the help and support of my editor, Jac Tobin. Her understanding of literature, and love of Wales, has provided me with a truly kindred spirit to work with.

I am grateful for the support of the following:

The former Ysgol Llangwm
The Rhug Estate
Criced Llanwrst
Popeth Cymraeg
Maerdy and Betws Gwerfyl Goch Churches

Marcie Layton, July 2021

Memories

Cwtch is a popular Welsh word meaning, in its smallest sense, a hug and, in its largest sense, a sanctuary or safe place. In the thirty odd years that we have owned *Cwm Llan*, our cottage in North Wales, it has been our cwtch. We have holidayed and lived here, raised our children and home-schooled here. When we were living and working in London, our hearts were here, and when we actually *were* here, it tore us to shreds to leave.

After my husband Peter retired, we moved here permanently with our two small boys, shedding our shiny city raincoats and leather shoes for green Barbours and muddy wellies.

I remember vividly the day when the headmistress of the boys' new school rang me in London and tried to talk me out of moving up here.

I think she thought we were nuts, leaving the capital city of England for a tiny rural hamlet in Wales.

I looked out of our kitchen window onto the herbaceously-bordered Ealing Green. It was warm and sunny, and big-bellied Heathrow airplanes were droning lazily overhead. On the kitchen blackboard we had written basic Welsh words, and we had stuck little Welsh post-it notes on everything else. We didn't know how to pronounce any of these words yet, but it seemed somehow like a head start to at least know what these words looked like.

Headmistress was cordial on the phone, cordial in the sense that, if someone had written out a transcript of our conversation it would be entirely politically correct and utterly harmless.

It was so incongruous, being in London, hearing a thick Welsh accent on the phone. Her voice was lyrical, a pure North Wales dialect, with none of the stammer of someone for whom English is a second language. But the tension resonating down the phone line was palpable. I could feel the stress and unhappiness emanating out of the receiver.

It threw me.

I hadn't expected that our dramatic Lifestyle Change could be seen as anything but wonderful in the eyes of – well - anybody that heard about it.

My education was just beginning.

She pointed out that the *ysgol* or school had about twenty-three children in it, mostly related to each other, and that all lessons were taught through the medium of Welsh. It was a very small, insular, close-knit community. By law, the school couldn't refuse us if we were in its catchment area, which we were, being a mere mile and a half from the centre of the village.

It hadn't crossed my mind that the school was a Welsh language school. I knew that the Welsh language was an integral part of life in the country, but I was incredibly naïve in those days, and I didn't realise that Welsh was still an active part of life for many Welsh people. I hadn't even realised that it was still taught in schools. I thought it was kept alive by those who wanted to maintain the traditions of the country.

I had some sort of moxie in me back then, the gutsy demeanour of someone who is just a little bit pig-headed, and undisciplined. I wanted to move to Cwm Llan, and that's what was going to happen. All obstacles would be overcome, no problem. My ignorance of Wales protected me from backing out; I could see no reason why this move wasn't a terribly exciting and wonderful adventure for me. For us. For the boys. For the village. For everybody.

By way of comparison, we arranged to visit a nearby public school as well, about forty minutes away. Our boys had started life enrolled in public schools, in London, and we wanted to have two different schools to visit before making up our minds.

We arrived in the rain. The public school was large, elegant, Virginia-creeper clad, ancient. The vines dripped large droplets onto us as we entered the impressive front porch. Everybody spoke English to us.

We waited, what seemed like an eternity. I had hoped that I could pull off two school visits in one afternoon without overtaxing the children. My concern was not about exhaustion; it was about high spirits. At last we were escorted down high-ceilinged corridors, bedecked with plaques honouring years of former students, cricketing achievements, and science awards. It all smelled faintly of cabbage.

We were suitably impressed, and a bit intimidated. It was also a boarding school, but we would take the option to arrange a rather long daily commute for the boys, an idea that didn't sit terribly well with me, but better than boarding.

Glyn was too young to start school. Dylan was the boy they were looking at. He looked pale, wide eyed, smaller than usual, as he quietly shuffled down the corridor trying not to make too much noise. He barely said a word the entire time. At last we were led into a special room, offered tea and a biscuit. Glyn, being younger and inclined to fidget, was nearly maxed-out on good behaviour and I could tell that soon he would begin to get lively.

Suddenly, the door burst open and a large man in army camouflage uniform stalked in. He had large black boots and a big barrel chest. Dylan nearly dropped his biscuit. Glyn stared, open-mouthed. My stomach clenched.

The large man spoke with a loud booming voice, telling us about the Army Cadet Corps at the school. I thought it very curious, the choice of this particular member of staff for our visit. Why were my two small boys being talked to by a military man? This wasn't a military school.

Maybe it was some sort of test. If it was, we were failing miserably. I had never met a soldier before, as far as I could remember. My father had been in the U.S. Navy, but that didn't really count. By the time I came along he had settled into the gentle paunch of middle age, and the only uniforms of his that I ever saw were old yellowing photographs on my parents' dressing table.

The man's uniform made me anxious and his voice made me recoil. Dylan wasn't listening, I could tell. He looked shrunken and even more pale, pressed up against the back of the chair seat. The fact that I was thinking about Dylan, and looking at Glyn, meant that I wasn't listening either. Peter was the only one in the family who didn't appear fazed by this encounter. He listened politely to the man, seemingly unaware of the timorous beasties sitting next to him.

After a suitably discreet period, we thanked everyone for our school tour, and said our goodbyes, explaining that we had another school appointment that afternoon. Dylan shuffled out hurriedly, staring at the floor. Glyn gave one backward glance at the large army man as he passed. I think he thought there was a war on.

We catapulted out into the rainy afternoon, glad of the fresh air and the cool rain. We'd had a long drive, a long visit, and now a forty-minute drive to the village school. I couldn't let the boys out for a run-around; it was too wet. They were bundled into the car, and I could see the temperature rising. They needed to offload excess energy, but there was nowhere to go.

I opted for complete transparency and begged them to be good at the next appointment. I explained that I realised how frustrating it must be, not being able to go outside and play, but on today of all days, we were all just going to have to be on our best behaviour. Weren't we?

I was a bit car sick by the time we reached Ysgol Llangwm. The windy Welsh roads, the shock of meeting the army man, and anxiety over the children's stress levels was beginning to take its toll.

We parked in the village car park, jogged quickly down the lane towards the school as the rain began to really hammer down. Glyn was beginning to giggle, and Dylan caught it too; both boys were wound up and raring to go.

The contrast between the two schools was marked. Ysgol Llangwm was a modest, pebble-dashed bungalow with two largish classrooms. There was a small reception area but for the most part it was open plan. Lessons were quietly going on as we entered; twenty-three pairs of eyes focused themselves on our entrance.

No teacher on earth could've competed for the children's attention, what with the four of us standing, dripping and puffing, in the lobby. The headmistress greeted us politely, gestured for us to hang up our sodden coats, and prepared to show us the school. There was no Virginia creeper, no cabbage, no scary army man. What we saw was a warm, friendly, happy building full of children, being taught by calm and motherly teachers, all of them women.

It was interesting meeting the headmistress now, after our edgy conversation on the phone. She was brisk and efficient; a petite, middle-aged brunette, speaking English quickly and Welsh even more quickly. She eyed me up when I entered, but if she had any misgivings, she wasn't letting on.

I didn't understand the words she spoke to the children, but I could sense from their demeanour that she ran a tight ship in that little building and took no prisoners. There was no mucking about in that school I could tell; I doubted there was even graffiti in the toilet stalls. But it wasn't an obedience borne of fear or intimidation. It was respect. The children and the other staff respected her authority and that was enough.

As we passed through the two classrooms, the children continued to stare unreprimanded. Dylan shyly inspected his shoes, but young Glyn, wound up incredibly tightly by the day's events, cut loose. I didn't notice him leave my side; I was too concerned that Dylan stay focused.

We looked at the brightly coloured class work on the walls, peered out the windows at the driving rain, smelled the faint remains of lunch, which wasn't at all unpleasant.

Next door we heard giggling, and then laughter. It swelled. Something was going on. That was when I noticed that Glyn was somewhere other than where he was supposed to be. He had decided to take his own tour and was ducking in and out of the rows of desks, having a glorious time. My car sickness turned to pure panic, as I hastily excused myself and went in pursuit.

Having at last cornered the culprit near the kitchen, we agreed that it was time to go.

It was a no-brainer. Hands down, we were going to enrol them in the little village school. We were going to commit, wholeheartedly, to the life of the village: the language, the farming, the mountains, the music, the small stone cottages and baleful sheep, the mud-spattered red tractors and tumbled down drystone walls. It was all so different. And so perfect. And it was about to become Us.

1
The Village

Cwm Llan lies hidden in the hills above Llangwm, a small hamlet of around 470 people. Llangwm lies just off the A5 trunk road between Holyhead and, well, the rest of the world really. Llangwm translates as "church in the bowl-shaped valley", or "village in the bowl-shaped valley", depending on who you talk to.

Our house's name is oddly enough the inversion of the name Llangwm. In Welsh the letter 'g' can mutate into a 'c'. "Llan" can also mean "a small-holding", so Cwm Llan could translate as: "small-holding in the bowl-shaped valley." Again, depending on who you talk to. Welsh placenames look intimidating on the page – such long words! – but actually they are purely descriptive. "The old summer place by the lake." "The big winter home". "Low-lying place in the meadow."

I mean this truly: it is the singer-not-the-song with Welsh translations. Our neighbouring house, *Ceseilgwm,* was rather endearingly translated by our neighbour Dafydd as "house in the valley which curves gently like the embrace of a mother holding her child." (This was poetically described, including gestures.) Another, more caustic fellow, translated it as "house in the armpit of the valley".

You always know where you are in Wales – literally – but it really depends on what aspect of the house the owner wants to describe when naming it.

Once we took a short term let on a newly restored little cottage named *Tegfan* (Pretty Place). The morning after our arrival we greeted the postman and introduced ourselves. He was looking baffled.

"I have some post here for you and the postcode's correct, but the house name is different."

"Oh really?" we asked. "What did it used to be?"

"As far as I know it's always been *Ty'n y Mynwent*. I wonder why your landlord's changed it?"

We shrugged our shoulders, went inside, and consulted our Welsh dictionary.

It became clear: truth in advertising. The house's name meant "Next to the Cemetery". And indeed it was. We had chosen to overlook that fact as the church was quite pretty and we couldn't really see the gravestones. I guess he thought he wouldn't be able to rent it with a name like that…

Llangwm has a deconsecrated Grade II listed Anglican church, St. Jerome's, and three very active nonconformist chapels, Capel y Groes, Gellioedd, and Cefn Nannau. No pub, and four places of worship.

Once, the school's headmistress asked parents to come up with an activity for the schoolchildren which was fun, educational, and didn't cost anything. I suggested a chapel walk. Each of the chapels made a special presentation of their own building, and we walked round the village to see them all. Many of the villagers had never set foot in other chapels apart from their own. They were each tall, well-lit buildings flooded with natural light, and surprisingly painted in delicate pastels, with brilliant white trim inside. The outsides were unpainted, dressed stone. The crisp white window frames and neatly painted front doors were in stark contrast with the Anglican St. Jerome's, which loomed darkly, devoid of white or cheering paintwork anywhere.

The Welsh and religion have a long and complex history together, which I daren't attempt to explain here. Suffice to say that these chapels are active, and essential to the life of the community. St. Jerome's languishes and rumour has it that it is available for a peppercorn rent from The Church of England in Wales, but it is a full-repairing lease, and it would take a strong heart and a deep pocket to bring it back to life.

The old pub is gone. It is now a staggeringly beautiful family home. The old post office is now a private home as well. The school is closed now, but the buildings remain: both the old schoolhouse, and the new schoolhouse, lie dormant.

When I first visited Llangwm, in the late 1980s, there was a so-called village shop, which upon inspection turned out to be the front sitting room of someone's house. Being painfully shy in new situations, I was hesitant about entering. Peter dragged me into the shop for Friday night provisions, and I peered meekly at one or two sparse rows of rather unimaginative tinned goods. I was fresh from sunny California, with its bountiful fields of fruit and vegetables, and I was hard pressed to find anything appetising for supper. I mourn the loss of this little shop now, as the nearest pint of milk is now in Cerrig-y-drudion, a town smaller than its name, which is fifteen minutes from our home, on a good day.

Llangwm is best known for its part in an uprising known as the Welsh Tithe Wars. Deio, a wise and weathered farmer down the lane, explained this event to me. He had a fabulous face, the sort of face you would expect to see in an edition of *National Geographic*. Years of exposure to the harsh Welsh weather had seamed his face into a million wrinkles. Across the bridge of his nose were the spidery traces of stiches, large stitches, handstitched by himself undoubtedly. I never got up the nerve to ask him the history of those stitches, and now I wish I had, as he has since departed us. When he told me about the Tithe Wars, he had a curious look in his eye that reminded me that the riots were very real, and very Welsh, and really did happen to the inhabitants of this place. I don't know how many current residents of the village have ancestors who died during this time but, as it took place in the mid-1800s, the descendants of this scandal are not too far removed from our modern day residents.

Historically, residents in Wales were required to pay tithes to the Anglican Church - one tenth of their annual income - whether they were church-goers or not. Although traditionally tithes had been paid in goods, the new tithe laws now demanded payment in cash.

As I have mentioned, in Llangwm there were three nonconformist chapels and only one church. The villagers as a whole attended chapel, not church, and didn't see why they should be paying tithes to the Anglican church. According to Deio, when the local villagers in Llangwm rebelled, the tithe collectors threw the rebellious villagers off the bridge on the 'Cwm Main' road, where they plummeted into the steep ravine below. Or possibly it was the other way round; I'm not sure now. He told me a very long time ago. Such a violent and turbulent time.

There is a stretch of disused road by this bridge, breathtakingly beautiful and popular with dogwalkers. I don't associate that spot with murder but perhaps I should.

Llangwm's pride and joy is its Male Voice Choir, who rehearse every Monday night in the village hall. The village car park is most days sparsely occupied, but on Monday nights it is stacked, two deep, with tractors, trucks and Land Rovers, and the most delicious choral sounds 'waft' around the village. The choir travels, and sings, and wins prizes, and has a CD or two. I wonder whether the daily hard work in the rough terrain of the mountainous hill farms and fields around Llangwm helps develop those powerful male voices.

Attached to the village hall, down a narrow inconspicuous lane, lay the school. Numbers had been dwindling, and the villagers could name precisely who was due to be enrolled, and when, and who was expecting a baby, and when.

The options for the school were bleak: merge with neighbouring Dinmael, in either one or other of the two school buildings, or close completely and everybody go to the larger school building in Cerrig-y-drudion. This would of course change everything: nobody could walk to school anymore, and life would become about buses and school carpools and no hanging around the school yard playing after school.

The schoolchildren didn't want to merge with Dinmael because they were rivals in all the local sporting activities. They certainly didn't want to merge with the much larger Cerrig either, for the same reason.

The tactic of keeping our heads down and not drawing attention to ourselves with the Local Educational Authority had been, so far, successful. Rumour had it that Ysgol y Parc, near Bala, was still open with twelve children, so there was hope for us. If the LEA was going to close anyone down, they'd most likely start with Parc.

Our boys had left before the school finally shut, so I'm not sure precisely what caused its closure. Neither Dinmael nor Llangwm was chosen in the end; the larger facility in Cerrig was chosen and so the dreaded bussing and carpooling began. The school building, football pitch, and playground look quiet and deserted; I think Ysgol Dinmael has become a private house. Probably named "The Old School House."

Although my family was foreign, and we were therefore outsiders, we were treated with consideration. I was always impressed when I walked up to a cluster of mums waiting for the school bell. As I approached, I could hear their Welsh conversation morph quietly into English, in order to include me. Often I would hear bi-lingual conversations, in which the speaker would seamlessly speak in Welsh to one or two people in the group, and switch to English when speaking to someone else. It was instinctive, and fluid; truly bilingual.

Before we enrolled the boys at the school, I had expected the schoolhouse to be a wonderful 19th century confection, with blackboards that squeaked and loos that smelled of Dettol. But when we first visited, on that incredibly rainy day, I discovered that this wasn't true. The current schoolhouse was a new build, with large windows, central heating that worked, and adjacent through a pass door to the local village hall. This hall was used for a variety of purposes, including the village choir, but it was the private domain of the school during weekdays. Lunches were also held there, so it was Mrs. Davies's domain as well.

Mrs. Davies was a legend in the village – she was the school's dinner lady – because she made freshly baked bread each day. She had snow white hair and a kindly face. Like clockwork, round about 11.00 each morning, she could be seen walking across the road from her little cottage to the school, a tidy little wicker basket draped over her arm, covered in a clean white cloth.

As I mentioned before, the 'old' schoolhouse lay in the centre of the village, with all of its faded Victorian charm, and outside loos. It had high windows, and no doubt the blackboards had *once* squeaked. It looked well-lit from outside but very cold.

I was entranced by the building. I had been thinking about running drama classes in the village, so when I was looking for a potential classroom, it was the obvious destination. I was directed to the owner of the building, an elderly couple whose house abutted the school building on one end. It seemed perfect for my needs, being quite close to the schoolhouse, so that children could walk to my drama classes straight after school without interrupting their parents.

But when I shyly knocked on the owners' door I was told that their grown children had bought the old schoolhouse for them – so that nobody else would buy it – and there it lay, chill and vacant, for years.

2
Cwm Llan

Oh, Cwm Llan. What a house. Coming upon Cwm Llan is like finding an uncut gemstone embedded in an ancient drystone wall. Just under two miles from the village, but a world away. On fine weather days we call it secluded, on bad weather days we call it remote.

As you turn off the A5 towards Llangwm village, your eye is drawn quite naturally up past the village into the hills, where our home lies. The valley is a perfect Welsh 'cwm', or bowl-shaped volcanic valley. Wales is peppered with v-shaped river valleys, gently curved glacial valleys, and round cwms, and so being in the cwm feels safe and protected, although its sheltering sides don't prevent foul weather dumping down on us from Foel Goch, rising steeply behind us. We're the only house in the whole of the valley. Just us, and the Jones's two ancient barns. Nothing else.

So hidden that most delivery drivers will tell you that they think they've gone wrong until right in front of the house.

From the village, you take the road, and then turn right at the chapel where the blue boat is stored, and past the barn where the corrugated roof is nearly off, past the wheelie bins bound to the fence with black plastic electrician's ties, past the third of several council grit boxes, up the lane and then past another grit box and up to the gate marked "Shut Me" – and please do – and then you see a cottage which is painted white, and then turn into a farm track and if you have a car that goes into 4x4 you should change gears now because you'll see a lot of gravel where the lane routinely washes away, and then the track becomes even more rutted because this is no longer 'council road' (it's down to us and the Jones family to maintain it which costs a bomb every time it does 'wash away') and then you carry on up keep climbing higher and just when you think there's nothing up there (although logic tells you that there must be something up there because otherwise why would there be a farm track?) you'll see a copse of trees and just past the hedgerows you'll see roof tops and chimneys, and suddenly there you are.

On a cold winter's night we will have left on the warm, golden sodium light, and the front porch light, to welcome you. During daytime, you will have the deadpan sheep and soaring, circling hawks to see you in. Be careful: mind the hedgerow down the last bit. It is an elderly hedge, tunnelled and worn by generations of ewes and their lambs. It is a favourite haunt of the sheep, for snoozing and for gossiping, but if you startle them they will belt out of the hedgerow in a panic, tearing their fleecy coats on the hawthorn and holly.

Cwm Llan lies on the lower slope of the cwm, so our garden is steep. The wooden gates guarding our drive are worn and tired. My sister carved a house sign for us, in Celtic lettering, which is weathered and greying, barely discernible. A bright copper beech hedge adds dash and colour, and by now it's so tall it provides us with complete privacy. The dried beech leaves rattle in the cold winter winds.

Cwm Llan is in the traditional late 19th century style. A carved plaque by the front door states **S.P.L. 1889**, although I'm not sure if it's stated proudly, as the local gossip in the village is that the aforementioned S.P.L. notoriously gambled away his assets, losing his land and his workers' cottages – including ours – and diminishing his estate somewhat.

Cwm Llan is made of undressed Welsh granite boulders, quarried from nearby Bala. The roof is slate, and mossy. The white flashings and window frames and front porch are tired and careworn.

Across the front of the house runs a stone terrace and, hidden behind more beech hedges, is a jacuzzi – bright blue and very incongruous – a nod to my Californian heritage. In winter we sit in the hot tub with champagne and toss snowballs at the cattle.

One frosty Christmas Eve I ventured out, late at night, for a festive dip before bed. I was clutching my swim towel around me and toeing carefully down the icy front steps, when suddenly half a dozen headlights began to pierce the chilly blackness.

The choir had come a-carolling.

Unbeknownst to me, they toured 'round the houses on Christmas Eve, raising funds for the local Air Ambulance, a much-needed emergency service in our remote area. I scarpered back up into the house, quick as I could, and dressed. The choir encircled our house with a mittened and bobble-hatted embrace. Their music was just achingly beautiful. The long Welsh vowels, so perfectly suited to music, rose and melted and charmed the very air around us, and instilled the most holy and sacred spirit inside of us. It was truly a silent night, a holy night, and all was calm and very bright.

We've made many alterations through the thirty years of our ownership, but it currently has three bedrooms, a big farmhouse kitchen, and in the den, a vast inglenook, which blazes merrily for much of the winter. Most of the alterations were made by one particular family of builders, who took great pride in their work and were excellent. In fact, so confident were they of their work, they were rather disapproving if we asked them to alter anything.

Once we asked them to take out a section of wall which had been put in by them, a few years back, so that we might put something else in its place. The brother who did the stonework, looked at me with a little twinkle in his eye.

"Oooh, you want that taken down, do you? I remember the day I built that wall. Ohh, it was cold. I was frozen stiff. My hands wouldn't work properly."

He was joking of course. Or was he?

The inglenook was the pride and joy of the house. When we first arrived, it had been filled in with an ancient Baxi boiler and wallpapered over, damp and peeling. It spanned nearly the entire width of the room which made us think there was probably something rather special behind it. We arranged for a large cast iron stove to be put in, hoping and praying that the removal of the earlier boiler would not collapse the house's end wall.

There was great excitement all round when the Baxi came out. A large recess was revealed, with two slate-capped plinths, a vast slate lintel, and an old cookpot bar embedded in the chimney flue. We had been warned that often fireplaces lost their ability to draw properly when the room was altered. Modern double-glazed windows and tightly sealed doors prevented the all-important drafts from fuelling the fire. Having pulled the Baxi out of the hearth, and knocked out an interior wall, there was plenty of ventilation and the chimney drew well.

Only once did the inglenook cause us any grief. We called it *Black Wednesday*.

It was winter, and we had been swimming at the public indoor pool in nearby Llanwrst. The weather had been on the turn, warning us of cold weather to come, but the boys decided to wear Crocs to the pool.

Peter had gone into town on an errand in his car, and I drove the boys in my car to meet up with him in the local playing field. The boys raced towards the playing field, damp and red-cheeked from the pool, when suddenly Dylan went flying and landed flat on his back. His Crocs had skidded into a path of icy mud. He lay there, stunned and gasping for breath. He was completely winded. Glyn giggled – he did look rather like a fish – and, after Peter arrived, he staggered to his feet and limped back to my car, nursing his injured pride. Peter still had shopping to do in town so we headed back home ahead of him. The higher we climbed towards Llangwm, the colder it got. Snow flurries began to skim the windscreen. The mountains ahead were turning white.

I glanced across at the boys' bare legs and Crocs, hoping that we could drive up the lane without having to abandon the car and walk. So despite the snow settling on the lane I tore up the hill as quickly as I could, trying to fly over the icy patches without stopping. Dylan got to 'Shut Me' gate, chilled to the bone, and when we arrived at the house, I bundled the boys into the house, gave them warm blankets and cocoa, and set about lighting the fire.

I had a small fire going when I noticed that we were out of our usual top-of-the-range house coal. I scrabbled around and found a bag of rather dubious looking lower grade coal which had been lurking in the hearth for a year or so.

The boys were cold. The house was cold. I was cold. I needed instant comfort, so I shook nearly the entire contents of the bag onto the fire and collapsed, exhausted, on the Chesterfield.

I dozed, and was nearly asleep, when through my half-closed eyelids I could see the comforting flames of the fire going up the chimney.

And flames in the fireplace coming down.

My eyes popped open. Flames shouldn't be coming *down* a chimney!

I stared at the hearth, mystified, as fingers of flame came creeping down out of the hearth, mingling curiously with the flames rising up from the bed of coal. It was raining fire inside the chimney.

Terrified, I rang Peter, who was driving back.

"It must be a chimney fire!" he guessed, the phone line crackling and intermittent.

"A what?" I shouted back down the phone, cursing my California heritage.

"A chimney fire. Something's burning inside the flue!"

By this time the boys had bundled downstairs and were gaping at the dramatic scene in front of them.

"What do I do? I don't know what to do!" I was in a blind panic, picturing the whole house going up in flames, surrounded by a snowstorm.

"Pour some water on it! I'll be home soon!" The phone line crackled again and he lost service.

"Dylan," I called out urgently, "sweetheart, please can you bring the hose up from the front garden? We have to spray water in the fireplace."

Glyn giggled with delight.

Dylan, now in his pyjamas and bedroom slippers, toed cautiously out the front door and down to the icy terrace below. He was gone longer than I expected; snow flurries were blowing into the house.

"Mummy!" he cried out from the terrace. "The hose is frozen!"

And indeed it was, unable to be coiled, or bent, or reduced in size in any way. Dylan staggered into the house hauling the stiff and frozen hose. Glyn squeaked.

Flames were beginning to rise out of the large mound of cheap coal; thick acrid smoke filled the room.

The smoke alarm went off. The dog cowered.

The boys were frightened now, really shaken. I tried to stay calm.

"Dylan, please can you go in the kitchen and get some hot water; we're going to have to thaw the hose."

I looked at him, worried; he was so frightened he couldn't think straight.

"I can't remember how to make the water hot," he said, scared out of his wits.

"With the kettle, honey, boil the water in the kettle!"

The dog barked and we heard crunching ice. Peter was back. The snow was falling heavily by now, and as I went to the front door to open the gates, the dog shot out into the snowstorm and straight down the drive towards the car.

"Stop! Peter!" I yelled, waving my arms. "Stop the car!" I pictured the dog dead under the car. Smoke poured out of the front room, snow billowed around the front of the house, Glyn was jumping on the hose trying to soften it. Peter stared up at the chaos with a stern expression.

He staggered quickly up to the house, took one look at the carnage, and said to me lightly, "Why didn't you use the fire extinguisher?"

It was a rather big learning curve we had that night: slippery Crocs, cheap coal, chimney fires, frozen hoses, disobedient dogs. It hadn't even crossed my mind to use the fire extinguisher. I'm not sure I actually know how. I was reminded of just how high up we really were. From the sunshine playing fields of Llanwrst to the snowy heights of Cwm Llan: it was a different world.

The house has a split personality. All of the rooms in the old part of the house are on the north side and are inclined to be small and cosy. The south facing rooms in the modern extension are bathed with as much sunlight as the sun can muster, considering we are deep in the cwm and prone to shadows.

Sitting on the terrace, mid-July, slurping ice creams, we can never believe that it will be winter. In mid-November, when the sun only just skims the top of the cwm and barely puts in an appearance, we never believe that summer will come again.

Much of the interior of the house is also undressed stone. When we bought the house, I had not long been in the U.K., and bare stone walls were to me the most beautiful and exotic thing on the planet, such a contrast to the particle board ranch-style houses of my childhood. We created for ourselves a moody and comforting house: stone floors, stone walls, a large black range cooker in the kitchen, thick curtains and soft rugs. Muddy dog paws and grit salt from the lane, coal dust and wood chippings: nothing can damage these slate floors. They just need a quick swab and they're fine.

3
The Farmyard

Below Cwm Llan lies the farmyard, spread out across the front of the house about six feet below us. It does not belong to us – the Jones family owns it – although once long ago, it belonged to Cwm Llan when it was a working farm. We watch the seasons change from this farmyard; it is a perfect metaphor for the agricultural year.

There used to be a lot more activity in the farmyard when Dafydd and his brother Deiniol farmed. They have both died, and Owain, the son, runs everything now.

Dafydd and Deiniol were twins, part of a large and prominent farming family down in the village. Dafydd was dark, lyrical, a pillar of the community. He had an air about him of one who could be consulted on just about anything, and whenever I had chats with him in the lane, I would come away with interesting information about Wales, farming, politics, whatever he had been musing about that morning. I suspect he was a splendid after-dinner speaker. He was a local legend because, although he was a sheep and cattle farmer, it was on a tour in Spain with the village choir that he was seriously injured by a bull, and the wound, even once healed, made him suffer acutely ever after.

Whenever I met Dafydd, I always had the slightly guilty feeling that I should be doing something useful. They worked so hard, the twins. The farming day is long, and the farming year is even longer. I often wondered what they thought of us, sitting on our terrace drinking coffee while they struggled with a stroppy sheep in the barn, or mended fences high up on the sides of the cwm in the rain.

Deiniol was smaller, darker, moodier, quieter. They weren't identical twins. He had a dry sense of humour, like his brother. I was never sure if he had a natural reticence, or if what I perceived to be shyness was the discomfort of speaking to me in English, his second language.

He had a very forgiving nature. I once brought a bag of chocolate Easter eggs down to them in the farmyard while he was moving the stock from one field to the next. I caught up with him at the gate into the farmyard. I opened the bag of eggs and he chose a few, leaning against the gatepost, chatting about the weather and lambing season. Unbeknownst to either of us the sheep merrily retraced their steps right back into the field which they had just vacated. He turned eventually, looked with mild surprise at the now empty field, and trudged off with his dog, munching the eggs, to begin the exercise all over again.

They both sang in the choir. We were very fortunate to have good neighbours, as much of the long lane was shared ownership and required our two families to respect each other and be considerate of its usage.

Back in the day when it was Dafydd and Deiniol who ran the farm, they used the farmyard for a variety of sheep-related activities. There was shearing, and scanning, and general fussing about with sheep on a regular basis. After weeks of solitude, the yard would suddenly burst into life, frothing with sheep one morning, and the accompanying cacophony was intense. They don't seem to shear up here anymore, although scanning still takes place a few times each year.

There are two barns opposite each other, both in a dubious state.

They are undressed stone, with slate roofs and Perspex sheets embedded in the roof tiles to light the interiors.

One barn had a small *ty bach*, or outdoor toilet, attached to it. This toilet was a two-seater, and the slate seat had two holes side by side, with no lid. There used to be small traces of sky-blue paint in it. I don't suppose the paint is still there now; I haven't peered in it for years. There was a tiny unglazed window, which for many years had two bottles mysteriously resting in it, the bottlecaps reflecting the car headlights at night like glowing sheep's eyes. I don't think it was an accident; it must have been a joke.

Occasionally as we passed it, a panicked sheep might burst out of it; I think they liked to shelter, or perhaps snooze in it, although it was rather small. It was a favourite with the curious lambs in particular. One or two sheep skulls littering the floor did not bode well.

Once we came home to find candy and Christmas wrap littering the yard. A delivery van had been, and – perhaps being new to the area and farming ways – the driver had delivered the parcel into the *ty bach* for safe keeping, not realizing that the local sheep population was a voracious and rather silly lot. They'd eat anything and were apparently very fond of imported American sweets. My sister was heartbroken, as I think she had invested a lot of time and effort into this care package from the States. I think perhaps I told her that it had been delivered to a barn, and not an outside toilet, to spare her further heartbreak.

Once, when the boys were small, possibly five and seven, I woke up one Saturday morning to the sound of manic sheep bleating, and sheep dogs barking. Sheepdogs are traditionally silent as the grave, so the sound of barking was cause for concern. Our bedroom was at the back of the house so I was a bit surprised that I could even hear anything going on in the farmyard.

I decided to investigate.

I peered out of the front bedroom window, and my heart stopped. Down in the yard, surrounded by white chaos, were my boys, running around in their pyjamas amongst the frenzied sheep, barking joyfully like dogs. Their little boys' pyjamas – cherry red, with little Christmas puddings on them – were complimented by *Thomas the Tank Engine* bedroom slippers, by now completely covered in sheep poo and oomska.

Why they weren't more terrified I'll never know. Dafydd and Deiniol were in the throng as well, bravely trying to control the situation, and their low-lying quivering sheepdogs were utterly baffled. Apart from the absurdity of the situation it was actually incredibly dangerous for the boys, being small of stature and no match for the force of the terrified ewes.

I belted down to the yard in my dressing gown. I wasn't quite sure where to begin: apologising to the Jones twins, extricating the boys, calming the sheep; it seemed like it all needed to be done at once, and I couldn't prioritise it all. The boys, ignorant of the dangers, were having the time of their lives. They were flushed and bright eyed, barking joyously and running like mad things, in and out of the woolly mass.

I caught Dafydd's eye first – he was not amused – so with a stricken countenance I uttered a hurried apology before grabbing the two plum-pudding-bedecked culprits and heading for the gate. The slippers were a write-off, the jammies went straight in the wash. But I couldn't bring myself to be too harsh with them as I was so grateful that they were safe and unharmed. Albeit a bit smelly.

A sombre, spidery, handwritten letter of apology was proffered by the boys. Two large chocolate Easter eggs by way of reply from Dafydd smoothed the troubled waters.

For a few years the barns were inhabited by a feral cat, who we assumed had been housed there to keep the rat population under control. She was a bitch of a beast, spitty and spikey, and we named her "Mrs. Woodbine", after a chain-smoking English teacher that Dylan had encountered during his brief incarceration in public school.

(He had written rather eloquently about some subject or other, and she had accused him of being a plagiarist. She didn't believe that some of the words he had chosen could have been written by a ten-year-old. We hauled the offending teacher up in front of the headmaster and did manage to extricate a grudging apology from her).

Naming a feral barn cat after her seemed reasonable revenge.

The barns were in a part of the farmyard sectioned off by two gates. An additional third gate at the entrance to the farmyard itself was only closed when work was going on. Cwm Llan was always secured with our own wooden gate, so when work was going on we needed to extract ourselves from the house by way of two gates in quick succession.

When the yard was full of sheep, they bleated and bawled with abandon, pushing and shoving and leaping into the air in a frenzy. Low and sylph-like sheepdogs darted in and out, policing the scene. Reversing our car into this mess was a nightmare. Work had to stop, the sheep had to be corralled, both gates had to be quickly opened and shut without any escapees.

Amazingly, I don't recall ever having any mishaps during this delicate negotiation. In fact, we seem to have maintained a delicate balance with the Joneses over the years. I ring down to their farm if I see any animals who need help; on snowy days their huge heavy tractor ploughs through the snowdrifts, delivering hay bales, allowing us access through the snow to the wider world. The most serious mishap really was the fault of a rogue delivery driver who left the gate into our garden open when he left. We arrived home to find a small herd of cattle greedily strimming our garden with their big, yellowing teeth. Even though it wasn't their fault, Dafydd and Deiniol apologised and speedily made good the damaged caused. They hadn't left the gate open, but they felt responsible. This was a perfect example of Welsh gentility, call it chapel upbringing or what you will, it was a consideration for others which I found repeatedly in our little community.

4
How It All Started

The most frequently asked question by newcomers to the house is: "How on earth did you find this place?"

When we were living in London, long before the children were born, we frequently booked holiday lets in North Wales. It can be a bit of a potluck finding a good holiday let, but we were for the most part lucky in our choices, as Peter knew what to look out for.

Even as far back as our still living in California I remember poring over the holiday let guides, shaking with excitement, reading in great detail every single listing, mouthing the names of the places silently to myself, curious how the names were pronounced. Glyndyfrdwy, Llidiart-y-Parc, Llanerchymedd, Pwllheli, Llanystumdwy, Machynlleth, Criccieth, Maentwrog: these were unbelievably magical and ancient names, so exotic to a California girl.

But once we booked an absolute duffer.

"Close to local amenities" meant there were huge electrical power pylons running across the property. The cottage was damp, chill, and dusty, making my asthma flare into a raging chest infection. After a sleepless night we decided to cut our losses and leave early.

On our way back to London, Peter said he wanted to show me an old cottage that he used to rent, on "winter let" terms of a fiver a month.

This cottage was in fact *Ceseilgwm*, and this how I first came to see Llangwm. As we drove up the windy track, we were met at the first gate by a man, clearly lost, with an estate agent's listing in his hand. He showed us a picture of a tumbled down cottage at a very low asking price. It wasn't anywhere that Peter recognised – it didn't look like Ceseilgwm – but I made a mental note of the estate agent's name before we carried on up the hill.

Ceseilgwm manages to look remarkably unchanged over the years. In photos that Peter took when he used to rent it in the 70s it looks precisely the same as it does today. We admired the pretty cottage in silence, and then Peter pointed out that further on up the valley there was another cottage; perhaps that might be the one in the estate agent listing.

At this time in my life I was painfully shy in the country. I worried about trespassing, and bulls in the field, and upsetting the locals, and all manner of imaginary scenarios that a girl raised on the California coast might have in a foreign country. I worried about going through closed gates, and I worried about taking photos at Ceseilgwm, and I worried about driving around the countryside looking for a cottage that matched the description of one I had seen only fleetingly in an estate agent listing.

But when we got back to London we contacted the agent, and he duly sent us a copy of the same listing. There were two reasons why the property was such good value. Firstly, the small stream running past the front door of the cottage swelled in the wintertime and had been systematically eating away at the foundations of the front sitting room. Ironically, although there was too much water in this part of the house, the second major problem with the house was that there was no running water. Plumbing in mains water meant gaining access over another farmer's land, and the word was that the farmer was not inclined to provide it, not being a fan, perhaps, of holidaymakers.

Almost as an afterthought, the agent mentioned that there was another property for sale, the cottage near Ceseilgwm which I had been too shy to visit. This was Cwm Llan. It had been a holiday let for an English family for over forty years, but the owner had developed Parkinson's, and they had decided, reluctantly, to sell it.

It had no phone, and rather creative but highly illegal electrical wiring. The water came from a small spring in the hillside behind the house. We asked for the estate agent listing and arranged to visit. We hadn't been in the market for a holiday let, but the pull was so strong, and the coincidences so coincidental, and the rental cottage had been so grotty, and Llangwm looked so charming, that we couldn't possibly say no.

The cottage was in a sorry state when we first saw it. A once cherished holiday home was mildewy, glacial, thick with dust and smelly. Apparently, the water from the spring was unreliable, particularly in the springtime when it was clogged with frogs' spawn. When the owners visited they drank a lot of beer! It was a traditional two up/two down configuration, with one of the bedrooms sub-divided into two smaller bedrooms so tiny that you could barely walk across the rooms if there were any furniture in them.

Well, I was besotted. My life had taken such exciting turns recently: we'd got married, left California, moved to London, and now were roaming the Welsh countryside. The prospect of a small cottage for weekend getaways was indescribably delicious.

We wheedled and cajoled the bank manager, trawled the listings for mortgage providers, and finally settled on a mortgage to buy the property, but with no spare change to do it up.

The weekend that we were due to exchange contracts we visited the house, and I in my enthusiasm took a sledgehammer to the wall dividing the two tiny bedrooms, intending to open it up into one bigger bedroom. After the first blow, a large hole appeared in the paper-thin wall. As expected, lathes and plaster were exposed, but something else as well. A previous resident had stuffed the walls with old newspaper clippings and Bibles from the 19th century.

We were speechless. We reached gingerly into the wall and extracted old chapel records, ladies dress adverts, newspapers, and Welsh Bibles, with children's names scrawled in pencil, in the margins. It appeared as if the previous owner had been responsible for the finances at the chapel at the bottom of the hill, Capel y Groes.

We had bought the cottage with contents, which were for the most part destined for the skip, but we had accidentally uncovered contents of a different sort: a small dusty treasure trove of local history. There was also an odd collection of household items, some of which were quite fun: a rather nice solid oak dining table, antique stone water bottles and, surprisingly, a pair of wooden Nordic style skis and poles.

We set about making plans and lists, utterly in love with the house and its future with us.

Back at our hotel that afternoon, we had disturbing news from the agent. My husband's face looked taut as he put down the phone after checking the messages.

"There's been a slight hitch," he said.

"What do you mean? What kind of a hitch?" I'd been dressing for dinner but froze in my tracks.

"The transfer didn't go for some reason, I dunno why, I need to speak with the bank manager."

"But: it's bank holiday weekend!" My leg began to jiggle nervously, under the dressing table.

"I know, I know, there's nothing I can do about it right now. Not 'til Tuesday at the earliest."

I felt slightly sick. "But I've just smashed the crap out of the bedroom wall with a sledgehammer."

He stared at me with a deadpan expression on his face. "Oops."

The property was not yet ours.

I felt weak, wondering if it were possible to patch up the hole in some way, very cleverly, so nobody would notice, if everything went pear-shaped.

It was an incredibly anxious weekend for us, not knowing if we were in fact going to be able to buy the house. By this time I couldn't imagine life without it, so this was agonising. But by the Tuesday the hiccup had been sorted, and the cottage was ours, and the yellowing books and papers which we had so carefully revealed, and laid neatly on the bed, could be examined and researched in earnest.

5
Early Years

Back in our London kitchen, looking over the well-manicured council-maintained gardens, we held the deeds in our hands. Our very own cottage. We were here, and it was there, but it was truly ours at last.

I will always remember the stark contrast between the two houses. How I could pack an overnight bag in London – the air balmy, hazy, slightly fuzzy round the edges – and after three-and-a-half hours on the motorway, when I got out to open the first gate, the sharp, fresh, untainted Welsh air would grab at me, punch me, stir my emotions and shake my body awake.

It was always a few degrees colder when I got out of the car. Shut Me gate was at the top of a very steep narrow bit of lane, exposed to the elements, with no shelter. You were literally stood standing out in the elements with no protection. The wind would slam down the cwm and knock you over if you weren't careful. The rusted gate would flip and shudder and fight your every attempt to keep it open for the car to pass through. It never just rained at Shut Me gate, it always poured.

In the early days we usually arrived in the dark, having left London after work and crawled up the M40 in whatever sort of commuter traffic was conspiring against us that day. The deep, black Welsh darkness at Shut Me gate was darker than any darkness I had ever experienced. No streetlights, no ambient lights, no house lights. Just blacker than black darkness, concealing large cow pats, small sheep pellets, mud, twigs, discarded fencing, rusted metal rubbish, ice, and all manner of things to trip me up as I struggled to open the gate.

Occasionally, if I happened to look up, I would be stunned by the enormity of the star-filled sky. It was an incredible sight. So many stars, which were hidden from us in London.

The bracing change in temperature slapped me quickly, so by the time I was back in the car I was wide awake and ready to unload everything at the house.

If we were lucky, the lane would still be intact. Often all it took was one raging downpour to get the soil moving, but equally an entire winter of rain/snow/thaw would erode the lane, shoving screeds of rocks and pebbles down it and into the rough verge. Deep rivulets and crevasses would slice down the hill.

It became a sort of living thing, that lane, a final steeplechase-style barrier between London and Cwm Llan.

Peter would have a sort of two-step with the car, trying to keep the wheels on top of the dirt track and not slip into either a crevasse or onto the slippery wet grass verge. In dry weather, the dirt became hard and unyielding, so the car wheels bounced uncomfortably through the potholes. In wet weather, the risk of slipping off the lane into the field was very real, and once you were into the mud, it was hell's own job to get yourself out again.

Ice and snow were a whole other kettle of fish. Sheet ice, black ice, snow drifts: it all converged on this little section of road and made everything ten times more difficult. When the snowploughs came they would plough up the council section of the lane to the end (which we were very grateful for, don't get me wrong) but at the end of the section the snowplough would leave the piled-high snow right in front of the access to our private stretch, making a snow drift deeper than anything they had previously ploughed. Got stuck in that a few times.

Cwm Llan in spring

Arriving at the house in the cwm

"Shut Me" Gate

Snow Lane

Winter snowfall in the farmyard

An old barn in the farmyard

Left: High summer in the garden
Right: The *ty bach* on a wintry day
Below: A warm late summer's day in the cwm

The lane after a rainstorm

Preparing hay bales for the winter

View from a window in the older part of the cottage

Once we were in a hurry, and just decided to wing it and go off piste diagonally across the field. We had a big, ancient rusting Isuzu at the time. We knew the fields around us fairly well and the field we decided to cross was reasonably flat and even. But we neglected to take into account the steep gully that the Joneses had dug out around the edge, to help with drainage. As we tried to breach the snow-filled gully, the weight of the car slammed us into the snowy bank. We were lucky the airbag didn't inflate. Amazingly, the engine was still running. Peter got out hurriedly and examined the front, buried as it was in the snowdrift. After about ten minutes of revving forwards and backwards, engine screaming, the mud-stained snow spewing out behind us, we finally managed to force the car up onto the road again. The car undercarriage never really recovered.

Twice we narrowly missed totalling the car in the lane. Once, when Peter had stayed in London, I arrived at the bottom of it with the boys. I saw large sprays of sheet ice splayed across from side to side. My experience of driving in snow and ice was nil. I was a timorous driver at the best of times, and I decided to take it slowly and cautiously. We began our ascent, and almost immediately the tires began to spin. I was driving a 4x4, a nippy little sport model, but with not much weight to it. I also had never used four-wheel drive before, and I wasn't exactly sure how to proceed.

The tyres spun, the edges of the ice churned up chips into the air, and after maybe ten feet the car began to slide backwards. I did all the wrong things, tried to brake, picturing us slamming into the steep bank, or rolling and crushing us inside. Somehow, magically, the car slid to a halt, and eased itself sideways. We were now at right angles to the lane, surrounded by ice on all sides, leaning precariously to one side. I wasn't strong enough to open the car door uphill, so we were forced to open the door downhill, stepping delicately out of the car hoping against hope that it wouldn't dislodge itself and roll over on us. We couldn't stand up, we couldn't grab the car for support, we had to half crawl half walk to safety at the bottom. I'm sure I was shouting and calling out to the boys – I'd never been so terrified – and the chaos attracted the attention of Deio up in his farm.

He calmed our frayed nerves and got the car to the top of the hill, without us in it. I was too frightened to get back inside the car; we walked. It was Deio who first explained the phrase to me, "Give it a bit o' wellie".

To his credit, he later rang the local Council Highways division and gave them merry hell about not gritting the lane. I don't think they realised that anybody was now living in Cwm Llan and I think they had given our lane a miss when they treated the roads.

I never forgot that incident, and whenever there was even the slightest hint of snow or ice I refused to drive, handing over all responsibility to Peter.

After several years, we had moved on from my jaunty little sport 4x4 to a seriously hefty Lexus, guaranteed to plough through the worst winter weather. On the second occasion all of us, including the dog, were making our way carefully down the lane, with Peter at the wheel. We had been advised to distribute our weight evenly throughout the car, but as we descended – me clutching the dashboard for dear life – the heavy car began to slip sideways, despite Peter's attempts to control it. We headed slowly for a snowbank, nudged into the gully, and began to slip sideways. I had my eyes firmly shut by now, but I could feel the weight of the car lurch to one side. Peter ordered all of us out of the car; a few inches more and we would have rolled. Somehow he managed to get it safely down, in some sort of free-fall with no control whatsoever.

Walking in snowy weather became my new favourite pastime.

All of our friends and family knew about the lane. It had the function of a weather report, whenever anybody came to visit.

"What's the weather like?" our London friends would say, as they were packing up their car for their visit.

"What's the lane like?" came next.

We had various little pit stops for people's cars, between the village and the house, gauged by their ability to manage the lane. Tough cars came to the house. Low slung cars parked at the end of the council road. Cheap cars with no horsepower to speak of parked in the village. We shuttled people up and down the lane in all weathers.

Dressing up and going out became less important in Wales, because whatever you did to yourself to make an effort and dress up was immediately obliterated by the challenge of getting down the lane in bad weather.

One of the highlights of the Christmas season was the Carol Concert at Rhug, a large historic estate outside Corwen. It was home to Marian, Lady Abertre, who had been married to an important member of the local landed gentry. Marian had dedicated her life to service, and was an integral part of the religious life, charities and fundraisers held in the North Wales area.

She had a cut glass accent, posh as posh could be, but was a warm and down-to-earth woman with a great sense of humour. She had a thick shock of iron grey hair, perfectly coiffed for social occasions, but I preferred to see it buffeted about in a high Welsh wind, as she marched around the ornamental lake with her spaniels.

The very first time I ever visited Rhug, I wasn't quite sure what to expect. We passed the entrance to the house regularly, as it was just off the main road, but it was set quite far back, up a long avenue bordered with tall trees. Even though I would always crane my neck to get a glimpse of the mansion from the main road, I would be lucky if I saw only the tops of the many chimneys briefly, and then only in winter when the trees were barren.

I was terribly excited as we turned into the drive, passed under the wrought iron arch emblazoned with the family crest, wound our way up the avenue, seeing tantalising glimpses of stone outbuildings on our way. We passed a walled orchard, a large courtyard which housed several stables, a clock tower, and several ancillary buildings, all designed in a chunky, granite, and heavy style.

I was delighted, however, upon arrival, to see Marian standing in the doorway of her Grade 1 listed mansion, holding a soup ladle, wearing a large oilcloth apron, surrounded by her wriggling spaniels.

Marian was a stickler for correctness: her manners were impeccable, her dinner table was always perfectly laid out, her social events ran like clockwork. Her faith was very important to her, and she was a key member of the Church of England in Wales, reliably in church every week without fail.

She was now widowed, and lived in the house by herself, while her stepson ran the estate. I was amused one day to find Rhug listed in a large picture book entitled **THE LOST HOUSES OF WALES**. She roared at this – Marian has a wonderful laugh – and said, "I'm not lost; I'm very much here!"

The house grounds were opened a few times during the year for fundraisers: a Bluebell Walk in early spring, and the carol concert. The concert took place in the estate's former chapel, now maintained by CADW (www.cadw.gov.wales), the Welsh organisation dedicated to the preservation of historical Welsh buildings and sites.

The farming estate at Rhug was a local legend, having converted entirely to organic farming methods, and having introduced bison to its livestock. In the early 1990s it opened a takeaway café from a small portacabin on the A5 trunkroad, and it had grown rapidly, adding a large and gracefully designed farm shop and restaurant. Today, Rhug supplies some of the finest Welsh meat products to local shops and as far afield as London.

A visit to its chapel was a privilege and a treat, as it was ancient, and elaborately decorated inside. The concerts took place entirely by candlelight. We decorated the building with festive greenery, and it was unforgettably atmospheric.

I enjoyed being asked to play carols on my flute for these services, standing high up in the minstrels' gallery at the back. A large and temperamental organ was also put to use, played by Billings, a friend of the family who travelled a great distance in all weathers to perform for them on special occasions.

The first time I played in the service, nerves got the better of me, and I rather unwisely forgot to compare notes with him about the carols we were about to play. It had been arranged that I would kick off the proceedings with a delicate solo rendition of *Oh Come, oh Come, Emmanuel,* to be joined by Billings in the second verse. At the appointed hour he took his seat at the organ. The polite chatter settled, and I began to play, the haunting and ancient melody floating high into the rafters through the candlelit shadows. The effect was unspeakably moving.

I finished my solo, and Billings prepared to join me for verse two, shuffling on the piano bench and flexing his fingers. Off he went, launching into an ebullient organ accompaniment – in a completely different key.

Even though I had started the piece, it somehow seemed like I was to blame. I struggled on valiantly, reading from my sheet music and noticing with distress that he was playing from memory, singing along in his own key with gusto. I had to stop; the effect was horrific. Billings won out and finished the piece with great aplomb. I backed into the shadows of the minstrels' gallery and hid, mortified, until everybody had left.

I was surprised when I was invited back the following year and made a point of pinning Billings to the wall until he agreed on a mutually beneficial key.

I had my special church clothes for these occasions, and a little black pair of suede ballet pumps which I saved For Best, and nice clothes with a sequin or two, maybe some velvet, or satin. But the lane took great delight in throwing up mud onto my trousers, sneaking rainwater inside my windswept raincoat and soaking me. My hair and makeup were a mess. After a while, I just didn't bother. I wore wellies down the hill and changed in the chapel car park. God wouldn't mind, I decided, if my sensible shoes replaced my For Best shoes.

After the concert, a supper was prepared in the big house, Rhug itself. Lady Marian presided, and it was well attended by people from all over: the estate manager, local vicars, other landed gentry, family, friends, Welsh learners, and us – the townies from London – muddy underfoot and glowing with delight.

No matter how much I came to love the countryside, and adjusted to the harsh winters, muddy lanes, and rural isolation, the suppers at Rhug could always reawaken the glamour I had previously felt in my London existence. I pulled out my festive best, tucked in the corner of my wardrobe and used only once, possibly twice a year. I rummaged around in the back of the bathroom drawer for ancient makeup and lipstick, tried to remember how to style my hair, and brought a can of hairspray in the glovebox to combat the effects of the lane.

Nothing quite describes a Georgian mansion dressed for a party. Light bounces off the gilt picture frames, winks in elegant chandeliers, casting a warm golden glow over the historic tapestried walls. An enormous log fire was kept fully ablaze throughout the evening. Festive greenery was everywhere. The murmur of voices was punctuated by laughter and the excited giggles of children. The very portraits themselves seemed to smile a bit more broadly, as the house was allowed to open up and show what it could do.

The food was incredible, prepared onsite by Marian's staff. Tray after tray of amazing canapés appeared in a steady stream through the doors, and you could always be guaranteed to sit next to someone very interesting and loads of fun.

The first time the boys were invited, Marian asked me what they would like to eat.

"Marcie, what shall I have Evelyn provide for the boys' supper?"

I thought of the fine wines, the elegant roasts, the elaborate vegetable dishes, and decided that I couldn't possibly coerce them into eating what the grownups were having.

"Um, well," I stammered, "they're not fussy. Just chicken nuggets and chips would be fine."

She looked at me, poker-faced, with a little twinkle in her eyes. "I'm not sure I know just exactly what a 'nugget' is."

I blushed and looked down, embarrassed that I should mention a word like nugget in a large organic farming estate. On the night, they were served with perfectly prepared roast chicken, potatoes and fresh vegetables, which disappeared down red lane in record time. Everybody sitting nearby pinched a bit.

One day, Marian taught me a valuable lesson in consideration.

She rang one sunny afternoon and asked us if the boys would like to come apple-picking. I was very excited, but a bit perplexed. I couldn't recall seeing an orchard anywhere on the estate.

The boys dutifully put on long trousers and sensible shoes, and we made our way to the Big House. Marian greeted us warmly and gestured across to a high stone wall in the Courtyard. We had passed this wall many times on the approach to the house but I didn't know what was on the other side. We went through a small wooden door and emerged into the most exquisite orchard I had ever seen. Trees of all varieties were laden and bending over with the sheer weight of all the apples. Nervy peahens, who had been quietly feeding beneath the trees, raised a terrible hue and cry, furious at having their supper interrupted.

Initially the boys were nervous about climbing the tall fruit ladders, but curiosity soon got the better of them and before I knew it they were high up in the canopy of the trees with bags, picking the fresh sun-warmed apples. We were soon swamped with apples, and yet it looked as if we'd barely made a dent. We staggered back to the car with our treasures, the boys grinning from ear to ear.

Marian met us in the doorway of the kitchen, smiling, wiping her hands on a dishtowel.

"Lovely, boys: you've done very well. That's quite an impressive assortment you have there."

They beamed.

"Now", she said, looking at them carefully, "have you picked any for me?"

The boys just stared at her, turning red, and then they turned and stared at me. I was red too, crimson down to my socks. It hadn't even crossed my mind to pick any for Marian.

"I'm afraid my apple-picking days are over," she continued, "I don't feel safe on a ladder".

I felt an uncomfortable cocktail of embarrassment and selfishness curdling in my stomach. Not only had I been selfish, I had allowed my boys be selfish as well. We all immediately dove into our sacks, trying to find the biggest shiniest apples for Marian. She waved her hand lightly.

"No, no, please take those, those are all for you. But I'll tell you what you can do for me. Let me show you my favourite tree. Right at the top, you should find some very nice ones."

We joined her as she walked, gripping a walking stick, back into the orchard. She pointed to one particular tree, a tall, straight, heavily laden tree, and smiled.

"That's my favourite tree. I love those apples. A few for my table would be perfect. Thank you."

The boys scrambled up the ladders again with new empty bags, daring each other to reach as far as they could into the boughs for every last apple they could find. I stood watching them and looking at Marian. She was incredibly fit for a woman in her seventies, courtesy of hours spent walking her dogs in the fresh air, but I could also see the fragility of a woman no longer prepared to climb a ladder and pick an apple.

I often think of that episode with the apples when I am around elderly people. I must really look at other people and see what they would like to do, what they are able to do, and what their limitations are. And whenever someone is generous to me, my first thought must be: what can I do for them in return?

Coming back to our little cottage felt like coming down to earth with a bump.

On arrival, after a long Friday night journey from London, Cwm Llan felt glacial, although in the summer months it might have the warm stuffiness of sunlight beating down on the wooden shutters all day. It would take a good three days to get it warm and welcoming, just about time for us to pack up and head back to London. This prompted my secret thoughts about moving here, imagining putting the suitcases under the bed, stoking the inglenook instead of closing it down, preparing slow-cooking stews instead of ready meals, and really, really, committing to the slow, rural, elemental life of North Wales.

Before we made the permanent move up here, we made several improvements to the house, in order to raise the general quality of life. Water, electricity, and phone were top of the list. We never met the previous owners, but from a phone call or two I had the impression of a gentle, kindly couple who were resigned, but heartbroken, to be giving up their once cherished holiday retreat. I thought of them whenever I picked the gooseberries in the front garden (sour as all get-out, add cups of sugar, always), the damsons off to the side of the house (best pierced and infused in brandy), and the Victoria plums next to the fence (soft, richly purple, not too sour but popular with the birds).

They may have left a legacy in the garden, but they left a legacy of a different sort inside the house. I'm trying to think of a way to describe the state of the electrics when we first arrived, and I think it's best to say, just picture the worst electrical wiring job ever and you wouldn't be far off. The lights would fuse when we turned them on. The lights would crackle when we turned them off. Sometimes the lights would fuse just for the fun of it. When we finally got in a local man to sort it, he regaled us with images of crossed wires, brittle and broken connections, and a completely unfathomable network of wires throughout the house making absolutely no logical sense whatsoever.

We began to seek out local builders and repairmen to come upgrade the house, which was a challenge during our weekend visits (who wants to work on a Saturday?), while leaving it to a longer holiday period causes its own set of problems (who wants to work during a holiday?) It was curate's egg-ish, the work force which we deployed. Some were brilliant, others, well, others we never actually saw, after numerous calls from London and frustrated trips up with no work accomplished.

The water system was alarming. It was a spring, from a hillside. We tried boiling it, filtering it, and finally ignoring it and bringing up our own drinking water. We had to come up with an equation whereby we invested just the right amount of money into making improvements on our second home, without crippling ourselves financially.

When the boys came along, it became increasingly difficult to manage weekends without a supply of fresh water. We were a mile or two from the nearest mains water supply, but it was suggested to us that we invest in a water bore hole on the property.

A firm was engaged from Yorkshire, and they dutifully arrived with enormous machines, drills, and unidentifiable objects needed to pierce and drill into the earth's crust. It looked like something out of a movie, the drilling operation. I half expected someone to shout that gold, or oil, had been discovered.

What did appear, rather suddenly, and alarmingly, was an enormous geyser of pure fresh Welsh water. It shot sky high, raining gracefully down to earth again, muddying the farmyard, alarming the sheep, frightening the dog, delighting the boys.

The geyser shot forth for days. A week. Ten days. It had "gone artesian". All we could do was wait for it to settle and flow in a manageable fashion. My imagination went wild, picturing the enormous water table beneath us and vast reserves of the freshest, untainted water, percolated through ancient rock and soft as silk. It was delicious. It was ours. It would be here, always.

Dodged a big bullet with the phone line.

We had been using a big heavy car phone (Millenials take note) which we brought into the house. It was about the size of a shoe box, and had a landline on it which you could plug in. This still required curling up next to the window in the sitting room, pressing your face right up against the glass, hoping and praying for a signal during good weather.

We finally got the phone company to agree to put in a landline. One morning as we were drinking our coffee, we saw two men with a large spool of phone wire making their way slowly across the field next to the house. They were good city boys, from Liverpool, and they marvelled at the scenery as they unrolled the phone line, occasionally stopping to take photos with their phones. I'm not sure how experienced they were at rural living. It was terribly exciting, but also worrying, as they stretched the line across the field at waist height. I didn't think the Joneses would find this amusing, and I didn't think it was too brilliant for the livestock either.

They reassured us that this was only a temporary measure, and amazingly, the line actually did work. But not for long. When we next came up, nothing was happening and the line was down. We delighted in guessing what had happened to the phone line. A rogue tractor? A ravenous sheep? A cow on the rampage? Weeks later the Liverpudlians appeared again, with special equipment to embed the line deep into the soil. Well, "deep" is a relative term. It unfortunately coincided with ploughing time, and the next time we arrived the line again was dead. After a third visit the engineer described to us a phone line which had been sheared in two. Or bitten.

The final visit from our Liverpudlian friends ensured a phone line which was deeply embedded. We paid the installation fee and were happily settling in, now connected to the outside world, when we got a phone call from the phone company.

"Hello then, y'alright?" The line still crackled on windy days but we could hear him.

"Yes, thank you, how can I help?"

"Ah, well, um, our lads, well they aren't really used to installing phone lines in the country."

"Ye-es?"

"And, well, they sort of missed out a few steps before installing your line."

"Ye-es?"

"Well, like I said, they're city lads and all, and they were supposed to get wayleaves across your neighbours land, and then pay for the right to cross their property.

"Ye-es".

"Which, um, they didn't, um, do."

"Right."

"And also, um..."

"There's more?" Peter sat down heavily on a kitchen chair.

"Yes, well, ah, there is a maximum distance we are allowed to travel when installing a phone line. If your property is further away than our maximum distance, we apply a surcharge for the additional distance."

Cwm Llan is two miles from the village.

"Oh. I see."

"Well, the good news is, we've done it now, and, like, we'll contact your neighbours and pay their wayleaves, but we installed your phone line without giving you a quotation first, so we'll be waiving the surcharge for the extra distance."

Peter and I sighed, loudly, together. "How much was that going to cost?"

"Oh um, well, about £10,000."

We stared at each other and did a little dance.

"Right. Well, that's fine then. Thank you for the work on the line; I hope it holds."

Peter hung up the phone and grinned. It was worth it, the crackling electrics, and the frog-spawned water supply, just to hear that the installation charge on our remote little cottage was the same as a connection charge for a semi in Basingstoke.

Over the years we have extended the house twice and bought a small bit of land out the back. A local family-run building company did the extensions. They had an understanding amongst them, a family of brothers, about who would do what; between them they covered all aspects of building work. I loved watching the stonemason at work, carefully picking out appropriately sized stone for the retaining walls in the garden and matching in the stone-fascia from the old house with the new.

His work was never random. He would carefully compose a wall of different shades of stone, ensuring there were no duplications too near each other. At first they all seemed like grey to me, but he pointed out subtle variations: pinky greys, bluey greys, brownish greys, which I hadn't appreciated until I saw them sitting next to each other. It made up a wall carefully constructed to look random. They sourced stone from a disused quarry in nearby Bala, to tie in with the original stone.

The carpenter would take elaborate measurements here at the house, disappear into his workshop back home, and reappear eventually with wonderful work in timber. Reclamation also proved helpful for us: our sitting room floorboards were reclaimed oak from a school gymnasium in America.

I remember one morning, tiptoeing across exposed joists in what was to be our new first-floor bedroom, but without any flooring. I took a carpenter's horse and gingerly placed it on two joists. I gazed out of the openings where the windows would go, too excited to breathe as I saw for the very first time what our bedroom view would be like. I squinted my eyes and tried to imagine being in bed, with a cup of coffee, looking out of those bedroom windows. I think about that moment often, when I wake up now, in our comfy brass bed, with warm duvets and fluffy pillows, and look out of those very windows, to the peaceful sheep-scattered fields beyond.

6
Welsh Lessons

We may not have realised how important it was for us to become Welsh Learners while we were living in London, but it became clear once we moved here that it was a very wise decision. Of course you can travel merrily through the country on holiday without having a word of Welsh, and pick up your *bara brith* and your Welsh cakes from a local corner shop entirely in English.

Deciphering placenames on a map can be tricky, and the computerised sat-nav will not help you there, as it often creates some sort of curious Welsh hybrid of names which mystifies English speakers and Welsh speakers alike.

But committing to life in Wales does become richer if you commit to the language as well. And as I've mentioned, it's such a beautiful and ancient language, colourful, descriptive, daunting, and sometimes ever-so-slightly irrational.

Before we actually arrived, we had a few weeks of commuting up from London so that Dylan could take Welsh Learner classes in the local school. They weren't going to throw him into the deep end after all.

Glyn was just old enough for the little *meithrin*, or preschool, so it was assumed that he would pick up his Welsh naturally. It turned out that the two boys each developed their own type of Welsh: Dylan's was more formal and grammatically correct, having had the classes, but Glyn's was more of a playground Welsh: colloquial, informal, regional.

This begged the question, for Peter and myself: how were we going to learn Welsh ourselves? The boys would be bringing home homework assignments in Welsh, be expected to read aloud to us in Welsh, and we were expected to help them with their reading of Welsh language literature.

We had made a few attempts to learn Welsh on our own, but really you can't fake it with Welsh: there are so many letters and sounds that are not the same in English – and don't even get me started on mutations, bane of my existence – and despite many hours in the car struggling with indecipherable Welsh language audio cassettes, we just couldn't crack it.

Luckily, help was at hand. *Popeth Cymraeg* (Welsh for All) is a company dedicated to just such a situation, and we were encouraged to join the local branch of their Welsh language classes, which took place in nearby Corwen.

I had never felt ostracised for not knowing Welsh. But we knew we needed to put a plan in place to learn the language, and we enrolled in the Corwen classes, not having a clue what to expect.

The lessons took place at Rhug, the aforementioned mansion on the outskirts of the town. The mansion, being very large and very grand, had enough space for a weekly class, so we all assembled in the dining room (not at the fabulous inlaid mechanised antique dining table, but at a smaller table by the window which only sat fourteen).

It was the most thrilling house.

I had difficulty concentrating when we were there. There was so much to see: swans gliding on the lake, Marian's spaniels wriggling and grinning and competing for your attention, the jaw-dropping beauty of the seasons changing in impeccably laid out gardens. The art collection was superb. The architecture of the property was exquisite.

It was like walking into a Merchant Ivory production.

Marian had many tales to tell of the house and its history, such as the bickering between the Georgian Society and the Victorian Society over who was going to be consulted on the restoration. She and her late husband had invested much time and money in the restoration of the house after they were married. Several obsolete Victorian outbuildings were taken down, restoring the exquisite Georgian balance to the core of the building. Most people arrived at the side of the house, parking under the open car port, but were you to wander in the gardens you would see tall Palladian columns proclaiming the entrance and taller-than-tall front doors which creaked open on the rare occasions when they were in use, flooding the exquisite front hall with glorious Welsh sunshine.

The formal reception rooms were a lesson in Georgian antique symmetry, bedecked with fabulous landscapes and portraits, but we all used to congregate during breaks in the high-ceilinged kitchen, warming ourselves in front of the enormous, ancient *Aga,* and watching wildlife in the garden out of the impossibly high Georgian windows. The kitchen was originally one of the formal reception rooms and had been cleverly converted so that the scale of the room remained, with its original decorative features. The end wall was devoted to a breath-taking art collection, all of them originals. There were many seascapes, and nautical themes, but my favourites were the animal sketches of Sir Kyffin Williams, my favourite Welsh artist and a good friend of Marian's before he passed.

Next to the kitchen was the housekeeper's pantry, and a small sitting room. There was always something interesting going on in the pantry, preparations for some party, or event on the estate, or often just fresh fruit being prepared from the orchard. I learned how to prepare raspberries from Evelyn, Marian's housekeeper: rinsing the berries carefully and laying them upside down, spaced evenly on kitchen towel, while they drained.

Our Welsh classes were taught by Mafyn, a cheerful, clever local woman with the patience of a saint. We always began our lessons with a rousing chorus of *Mae Hen Wlad Fy Nhadau* (Land of My Fathers), followed by a cheeky rendition of *Sospan Fach* (Little Pan). We had a specific curriculum to follow – which Mafyn adhered to – but she gave us enough free rein to bring in material of our own, amidst much good humour and joshing.

Once, at Easter time, we hid Easter eggs all over the ground floor, and then as we ate them we described in Welsh where we'd found them. (*The green egg was under the settee. The blue egg was on top of the portrait*). At Christmas time I filled a large sack with all sorts of clothing, which we took turns dipping into, blindfolded, and dressing ourselves. We then described what we were wearing (*I am wearing a leopard-print scarf, a pink velvet hat, sunglasses, and blue gloves*). Our vocabulary grew, and we were encouraged to use our Welsh on a daily basis.

Laughter was a constant in these lessons. We were a good-humoured mix of members of the local clergy, retirees, and local businesspeople. We would revel in each other's successes and failures with the language, but nothing compared to the class before *Noson Guto Fawkes*, or Guy Fawkes Night.

We had been discussing how to make an effigy of Guy Fawkes to burn on the night, and Mafyn was providing us with translation.

I asked her: "Mafyn, how do you say 'hair' in Welsh?

"Gwallt," she replied. We scribbled it down in our notebooks.

"How do you say "straw"? I added.

"Gwellt." We began to snigger.

My eyes lit up as I suddenly remembered a word which I'd translated earlier in the week.

"Can I just check: how do you say 'wild'?" Mafyn's eyes met mine, and the corners of her eyes crinkled in merriment.

"Gwyllt!"

We were on the floor. Weak with laughter. In order to make an effigy of Guto Fawkes you needed – wait for it – gwyllt gwellt gwallt!

I committed more crimes against the language than anybody else. I asked for a dozen English at the butchers (*selsig* is "sausage" but *saesneg* is "English"). I asked for a pint of milk in my tank at the petrol station (*llaeth* is milk but *llawn* is full up). There was a genuine appreciation for anyone who was a Welsh learner, and although I never achieved any level of sophistication I was able to book-end my conversations in Welsh, and was pretty good at deciphering place names, as they are always descriptive.

Marian was great fun to be with, and I have many happy memories of days and evenings spent at the mansion. I never set foot upstairs. However, the rest of the grounds were a rather elegant adventure playground for all of us. The boys played cricket on the lawn and climbed the ancient grassed-over icehouse. A dog walk round the lake took at least forty minutes, and worked up a hearty appetite, usually leaving me breathless.

Her late husband had been in the Navy, which was reflected in the presence of small heavy black iron cannons, positioned at intervals around the garden; perfect for hiding Easter eggs. Once, after a particularly animated visit, Marian rang me to enquire had either of the boys moved the cannon balls which were stacked neatly outside of her back door. Glyn was the culprit. He also became notorious for hiding the key to the downstairs WC. He worried that Dylan was going to lock him inside, so he hid the key while he was in the loo and forgot to put the key back in the keyhole. Marian took these pranks in her stride: she might sound stentorian on the phone but it was a good-humoured, tongue-in-cheek sort of stentorian.

It was another world. It was a beautiful world. It wasn't my world, but it was a lovely place to visit.

7
Cricket

Cricket is not normally associated with Wales. There is a professional international team, based in Glamorgan, and many amateur teams dotted throughout the country, but mostly Wales is a rugby and footballing nation.

Peter taught our boys cricket from a very early age, when we were still in London. Dylan remembers bouncing up and down on the sofa in London, waving a bat about. Whenever he saw the slo-mo action replays on television, he thought he was supposed to bat slowly as well, and he awkwardly waved the bat across in a gentle sweep, languidly.

It's a long game, with expensive kit, and an elaborate maze of rules. Our boys and Peter really bonded over cricket, and when we moved to Wales they played for a local club about half an hour from the house.

Saturdays were given over to cricket. All day. Sometimes Sundays and midweeks as well. It was more difficult to play cricket, based where we were, because there wasn't much of it about, but the positive side was that there weren't a vast number of players in the club and our boys had many, many opportunities to play. At their peak they both played for the First XI, the Second XI, three Junior teams, the mid-week Senior team, and the County team, *Eryri*.

That meant quite a lot of commuting, but the journeys were beautiful, and the cricket grounds usually were as well. It was like a mini break, travelling to these matches, through the loveliest parts of North, Mid, and South Wales.

Some grounds were buried deep in towns and cities, and others were on borrowed farmland, or in the back gardens of country estates. One ground was notorious for not having proper ground covers (tarpaulins were all they could manage), and for having a healthy wasp community in the outdoor loo.

The cricket teas varied widely: some positively cornucopia-like, and others very spartan. They were the subject of much discussion in the pavilion beforehand. The middling teas usually consisted of the obligatory sausage roll, pizza slices, coleslaw, cocktail sausages, slightly curled sandwiches with various fillings, and store-bought puddings which looked rich and inviting on the table, but hit you like a Mack truck late in the afternoon when players began to get sleepy. There were rumours of cricket tea sabotage: offering heavy-to-digest meals like chilli and lasagne to a team who was going to be in the outfield, in the heat, for a couple of hours straight.

When I initially got involved in the world of Welsh cricket, I fussed and worried about the incredibly unhealthy content of these cricket teas. I imagined that, because cricket was a sport, healthy food would be on offer to allow people to play at their best.

I was disabused of this on several occasions. For many players, I was assured, they were only in it for the teas. A sunny weekend spent tanning yourself on a cricket pitch and eating pizza, sausages, and trifle was, for many, Nirvana.

Dylan would pace and fuss and fume the night before, scanning the cricket results from other teams and obsessing about the teams and the running order. Glyn, more phlegmatic and of a calmer nature, didn't give it a second thought. I would prepare elaborate picnics for the day which needed to provide enough food for the entire family, for at least two meals, because we would often arrive just before noon and not leave the ground until it was nearly dark. Even though our lads were invited to partake of the cricket teas provided by the clubs, they had a habit of wandering towards the car, late afternoon, wistfully eyeing the contents of our picnic basket and hoping for leftovers.

In the morning, I had the twin stressors of prodding Glyn out of bed late, and calming Dylan down early; he would be pacing the floor and air bowling from early morning.

The cricketing community really helped ease our boys gently into the local secondary school, when they finished home education[1] and returned to mainstream school to prepare for their exams. Virtually the entire club was there, and on the first day in their new school the boys were so excited to walk down the corridors, being given high fives and cheerful greetings from their teammates as they passed. Dylan once bowled out the headmaster in Bodedern, during a Senior's match, and anxiously wondered if it would affect his standing in the school. It didn't.

---

[1] Having moved house and changed schools, both boys were found to have Special Educational Needs. We made the decision to home-educate them until they were ready to prepare for university entrance exams. This chapter in our lives is covered in detail in my first book, *A Life Lived Behind Glass*.

8

Eisteddfods, the Urdd and the Deinosor

If Welsh is the garden of Wales, then the Eisteddfods are the spade and the hoe, cultivating and nurturing the country with their creativity and their passion for the arts. They run annually, and are extremely popular, with attendances running into the thousands each year.

The earliest known eisteddfod was held in the 12th century, but an 18th century resurgence gave eisteddfods the image they have today, with the crowning of the Bard, the Bard's chair, and special Bardic names. The word derives from the Welsh verbs *eistedd,* to sit and *fod,* to be. Sitting all together is the resulting meaning. In fact there is a legendary comment from a small Welsh child, during competition, "Why are they called *eisteddfods* when all we do is stand up?"

For a country with so many remote farmsteads and rural lifestyles, eisteddfods are the perfect opportunity for families and friends to get together socially, have a holiday perhaps, travel to each new location with a caravan or tent, and take a break from life's routines. The Welsh language is at the core of these festivals and is probably single-handedly the primary reason why the Welsh language survives today, is taught in schools, and is seen everywhere you go on signposts and in restaurants and literature.

Participants must either live in Wales, have been born in Wales, have one or both parents who have been born in Wales, or speak/write in Welsh. Both of my children participated in the Urdd eisteddfods, open to all children up to the age of twenty-five. They were involved through Ysgol Llangwm and travelled to various parts of Wales each year for competitions, if their school got through to the finals. "Seeing the stage" is the coveted final step for those who compete in the finals. Winning is the goal, but for many, the sheer excitement of the whole journey and participation with friends and families, is key.

There are three types of eisteddfod in modern Wales. The largest is the International Eisteddfod, which is held each year in July, in Llangollen (*international-eisteddfod.co.uk*). Also held annually are the National Eisteddfods (*eisteddfod.wales*), held in North, Mid, and South Wales, in rotation, and in different towns and cities. The Urdd is the annual Youth Eisteddfod (*www.urdd.cymru*), also held in different places each year, and involving schools and clubs as well as individual participants.

Having been raised in California, I'd never experienced anything like them. California is twenty times larger than the whole of the country of Wales, and certainly didn't host national arts festivals. The National Eisteddfod runs for eight days and is the largest music and poetry festival in Europe.

The sheer scale of these festivals is incredible. They must provide performance areas, stalls, food, campsites, car parking, open-air entertainment venues, etc. Although competition is at its heart, the spirit and bonhomie I've experienced is refreshing. It feels very safe to let your children run around with their friends, seeing the sights; a wonderful way to have a childhood.

Many Welsh children I've met have incredible poise and confidence onstage, as a result of performing and competing from an early age. It is instilled in them at school, in local choirs, chapel, and social clubs.

It is a serious commitment for any town, hosting the National or the Urdd. All eyes are on the selected venue from the minute it is chosen; often people's summer holidays are centred around the events. I can't think of many other countries who host an arts festival on this scale, and entirely in a native language. It is an example of how national pride can be sustained creatively and artistically, not just politically.

And meddle with National Pride at your peril…I wrote the following account of Glyn's own eisteddfod experience for a short story anthology: *Zero Hours on the Boulevard* published by *Parthian Books.*

Fi 'di'r Deinosor

…MY SON WAS IN AN eisteddfod. Well, sort of. He was in the first round of prelims for one. That hardly counts. He was about as far away from 'seeing the stage' as a penguin is from seeing Texas.

And he was dressed as a dinosaur.

His primary school was very keen on eisteddfods, and there was much fervour and anticipation about these events. Everything, and everyone, was thrown into the pot: *dawnsio gwerin*, crafts, recitation, choirs, art, everything. Someone once advised me to find a craft option that wasn't very popular, like puppetry, and go for it; it was a sure way to get through the first prelim. (Mind you, I was given this very same piece of advice about entering the village fair in August: find an obscure vegetable category and go for it).

Now, I had seen the prelims for these events before, and it seemed to me that everybody was being coached to do precisely the same thing, in precisely the same way, and I didn't see how anybody could possibly tell the difference when it came time to adjudicate them.

I was not a sheep. I wanted my son to be different.

He was taking singing lessons at this time, at the tender age of eight, with a wonderful, fun-loving singing teacher who was no stranger to eisteddfods herself. She had told me what song was going to be sung: a chirpy little number about a dinosaur and his little dinosaur antics. We agreed that she would coach him on it instead of the teacher at the primary school.

We had the costume from a long way back; I think it came from the Disney Store. It was large, full- body creation: green, and scaly, and vaguely, mildly, authentic-looking. We're not talking Barney here, is my point. It had a thick, swishy tail, and a big pot belly, and when your mum or dad zipped you into it, you couldn't escape without help. The dinosaur head sat on top of your own head like a crown, and your face peered out roughly where the throat should be. The feet were big, padded claws with elasticated straps that hid your shoes, and collected all sorts of bits of rubbish wherever you walked.

Well, I got my little lad into this creation and we began to work on a surprise for the singing teacher.

All the other children we'd seen rehearsing this song stood calmly, singing their little hearts out to the FIRE EXIT sign at the back of the school hall. Their eyes popped open unnaturally wide, and they would barely move a muscle, save for the in/out/in/out of their little ribs heaving as they sang.

I got my son to do a few little gestures, to support the lyrics: a little kick here, a little teeth brushing there. At one point, I got him to do a big 'ROAR' that he performed with great gusto. We hid the costume when we got to the music lesson, and, giggling nervously, I asked the teacher to wait briefly while we prepared ourselves 'backstage' in her front hall.

Her face was a picture when we came into her front room and she saw the costume. My son looked both delighted and mortified at the same time. The room shuddered with good humour as he stood there, being admired. This was nothing compared to the response when he began to sing. The little kicks and gestures went well. The teeth brushing was cute. When the little roar came out his teacher let out an exclamation that was just delicious! I'm not sure she'd ever seen anything like it, at least not in her front room.

We all fell about when he'd finished and I thought to myself: I am NOT a SHEEP! Dare to be different!! I asked her what she thought and reminded her that I'd had no experience of these things. Could we pull it off?

We had some discussion about whether or not it would work. She brought her husband down from the office in their loft conversion, and he also had the marvellous double-whammy reaction: first to the costume, then to the song with its little bit extra.

What a high! I felt cute, I felt clever! I felt daring, and original. My son was getting a bit fidgety in the costume, and I thought perhaps he needed the loo, so he was extracted, like some sort of curious caterpillar, from his padded monstrosity.

Over the coming weeks we worked on this risky new take on traditional Welsh musical form. I was getting rather sick of the song, but on we bashed. His teacher's daughter, a choir conductor in the local church, came over and listened to it, and there was much giggling and fidgeting and bonhomie in the lessons.

Finally, the big day arrived, but there was trouble in Paradise. Someone didn't want to wear the costume. Someone had been watching rehearsals at school, and nobody else was wearing a costume. Someone was worried about looking silly

The heat was on from my end, as well, because the parents had been asked to 'volunteer' for various jobs during the trials, and I got volunteered for "Cash Box on the Lunch Queue". This meant that when all of the competitors, and their parents, and the adjudicators, had their lunch breaks, they would take a tray in an orderly fashion, pick up their food of choice, and hand me their money at end of the queue. I had to make change in the Urdd's little metal cash box.

Now, maths is not my strong suit, and my Welsh is even worse, but for some reason (perhaps, because it's about The Language, stupid) I felt compelled to wade through these transactions in Welsh. I was dreading it, and left for the village hall muttering *"un, dau, tri, pedwar"* in a state of ever-increasing anxiety.

Well, the music prelim came first, and it was not a pretty sight. A cold, lino-encrusted classroom had been filled with cold plastic chairs, and a cold, wood-veneered table, and the view to the outside car park was cold and grey.

Warm, comfortable and thick-waisted mums padded about with their warm and comfortable children, murmuring gently in Welsh to each other, and there was a lot of hugging and gentle guiding of performers into their little rooms.

We, however, stood shivering in the cold corridor, and argued, ***sotto voce***. My son was tortured. He did NOT want to wear the costume. He tried alternately pleading, and demanding, not to wear the costume.

I ganged up on him with the ammunition that Daddy, and Mummy, and Teacher, and Teacher's Husband from the office loft conversion, and Teacher's Daughter the conductor from the local choir, all had seen the dinosaur costume and thought it was wonderful. We were not SHEEP. We dared to be different. He WOULD wear the costume.

I really don't know what the hell I was thinking.

Anyway, I stuffed him into the costume, like too many bags in the bin on the night before rubbish collection. We waited in the corridor, and every child who passed by stared, and then grinned, and sniggered at us, and then quickened his pace, as if to race off and tell as many children as possible that there was a dinosaur in the corridor, preparing to sing.

It was our turn. We tiptoed nervously into the room. The adjudicators went deadpan. The other children gaped. My son tried to say his name, whispering in terror from the larynx of the dinosaur. The accompanist was a portrait: not a twitch of a smile.

The music began, and my son inched forward. We could barely hear him. He started to do his little kick but thought better of it, or maybe, he was too busy being mortified to remember to do it. He forgot the words. He stammered. The tail shuffled around the floor morosely, gathering any bits of dust and rubbish that the elasticized feet had left behind.

I tried to get him out of there as quickly as possible afterwards. Did I imagine this, or did we both try to go through the door at the same time, Mummy and dinosaur, competing for space and bumping into each other, and getting ever so slightly stuck on departure?

There was retribution. Big time. Nothing I said helped. It was disaster from start to finish. I was sure he hated me, and the costume, and the song, and singing, and the cold room, and the deadpan adjudicators, and anything else associated with that particular day in Wales.

He went home with Daddy, and I stayed on. I had "Cash Box on the Lunch Queue." Oh goody.

I'm not exactly sure how many people got short-changed during that lunch break, but I only hope I erred in favour of the Urdd. I can't count, in any language. At least I could devote my full attention to the little compartments of change in the cash box, because I was determined not to make eye contact with anyone. I couldn't bear to see the memory of the little dinosaur reflected in their eyes. The slightest hint of a giggle would've pushed me over the edge. I may even have short-changed the adjudicators, I don't know; I didn't look up at anyone, at all, ever.

After about the first transaction I gave up on the *un-dau-tri-pedwar* thing as well, because, honestly, who was I kidding? I wasn't Welsh. I never would be. I was just a foreigner: a very, very foolish English-speaking mother with a tear-stained child in a dinosaur costume.

It all came to a head in the *Spar* shop, down the aisle where the really cheap sweets were. I don't mean where the big boxes of *Celebrations* chocolates and the posh-sounding dark chocolate *Bourneville* bars were stacked. I mean down where the red liquorice whips were, the jaw breakers, the oddly coloured gummy things, and the left-over Easter sweets on the cusp of exceeding their sell-by dates.

I was in pain from pent up emotion. My throat ached from supressed unhappiness. I had the mother of all headaches, and of course this is precisely when you remember that you've run out of milk at home, and even though the wisest thing would've been to go home and go to bed, I had to get a pint of milk from the Spar shop.

I sloped down the aisle, hoping not to see anyone, with two big 3-litre jugs so I didn't have to go back there for at least a month. Suddenly, from behind the *Walkers Big Eats*, 'Aunti' Gwyneth said *hello. How was I? How was the family?*

It was all too much. I opened my mouth, and tears came out. They leaked down through the laughter lines around my eyes and dribbled into my shirt collar. I tried to sound perky, or polite, or, even at this point, sounding like a NORMAL person would've helped, but it was very clear that I was in great distress. I was crying dinosaur tears.

I was crying for myself, and my little boy, and for Wales, and for the po-faced adjudicators, and for all the people who I'd short-changed in the lunch queue. I cried for the fun-loving singing teacher, and her fun-loving family, and for Aunti Gwynedd who had to stand there with her cabbage and her thick-cut marmalade and her *Denbighshire Free Press*, asking if I was all right.

It's been four years now, since the Year of the Deinosor. My son used to remind me of the incident on a regular basis, and it never failed to push all of the most important guilty parent buttons in me. He doesn't mention it quite so much now. I think my penance is nearly over; probably one or two more years and I should be reprieved. We've moved house, and he's got a different singing teacher now. He sings scales with funny vowel sounds, and arias in Italian. I think, perhaps, his dinosaur years are over...

9
Sioe Season

The summer months were a time to work hard and play hard in the farming community. We watched it daily from our little cwtch. There were endless rounds of shearing, hay baling, fencing, and all manner of things involving sheep bleating madly away in the farmyard enclosure. The heat would dry and crack the soil, stream beds would shrink, flies and dust would pester the livestock. As we drove up the long track to the house, we were slammed back and forth against the side of the car, because the mud puddles of winter went hard, and the old tyre tracks through the mud became ridges of baked clay, so driving over the potholes was a nightmare. Heavily coated sheep lay collapsed in the shade of the rowan trees and hawthorn hedgerows. They would glance at us as we passed, panting, hoping we weren't there to move them along into the next field, or chase them about with sheepdogs.

Each of the little towns and villages near us used to have their own summer fete, their local *sioe*. You could literally attend one each weekend for nearly two months, and that didn't include the Royal Welsh Show in mid-Wales, or the Anglesey show. For children out of school, this was a lifesaver. Many children helped out on the farm every day and socialised through the *Welsh Young Farmers* and by going to the local shows.

Sioe Llangwm was a modest affair, much loved by the village. It traditionally took place on the August bank holiday weekend, one of the last of the year. Sheep would be groomed, and penned, chewing their prize rosettes lazily. Baked goods competed for prizes also, as did individual fruit and vegetable offerings. I just loved the feeling of the place: happy kids, relaxed and laughing parents, the hot summer buzz of insects and birds calling. Children were in and out of each other's houses all day, visiting aunties, uncles, cousins, nieces and nephews, babies, puppies, new kittens, baby ducks, prize heifers. It was timeless. It was priceless. I wish I could capture and store the lifestyle somehow, but things change and the old ways disappear.

The Jones's farmyard is used less and less, as young Owain, now in his thirties, uses modern and more efficient ways to raise his livestock. We still see the streaming of sheep being herded from one field to another, a small black dot of a dog guiding them seamlessly across the hills. They move as gracefully as a murmuration of starlings.

By late summer the house martins have abandoned their nests, and the annual battle begins to crack and break down their clay caves, trying new methods each year to prevent their nesting again in the eves. It's a messy business. The most successful – albeit unsightly – method was to hang bright and shiny CDs under the eaves. The presence of a two-disc set of "Barry Manilow's Greatest Hits" was enough to scare off the birds, if only to find an alternative place to nest on the opposite side of the house." They were extremely fond of Cwm Llan and its peaceful garden. Food and drink were always at risk below.

The boys used to love the hay bales. We had clues that it was nearing hay baling when the huge machines would arrive to cut and turn the hay, making cryptic patterns in the grass. Although it was nothing to do with me, I fretted about thunderstorms in the days between the cutting and the baling. Before the crops were even cut, a single day's wet and windy weather could ruin them, snapping and scattering the slender stalks with the force of a high wind.

The hay baling day was a long and hot one. Dust covered everything in sight, and the tractors droned lazily up and down, up and down, carting the bales back behind the barns for winter feed. That never changes. The hay bales are stacked neatly and high, traditionally, every year. Woe betide any small boy whose cricket ball ended up in the hay bales. It was lost until next spring when the supply had dwindled to a manageable height for search and rescue.

Once, Headmistress gave a homework assignment to the children, asking them to describe the farming year. She suggested that if they weren't sure of something, they should ask their parents. Our boys dutifully brought the assignment home, and we all sat round the kitchen table writing about what we remembered having happened throughout the previous year. I didn't think I'd done too badly – in fact not bad at all for a girl from Southern California – but we must've been wide of the mark. When the boys' assignments came back there was no grade, merely the cryptic remark: "Ask a farmer!"

10
Cwtch

We hadn't intended Cwm Llan to be our *cwtch* when we first bought it. It just seemed essential to have it in our lives. I'd never even heard of the word and would've struggled to pronounce it properly.

We retreated there after chaotic working weeks in London. When our children were small it became an unofficial babysitter, nurturing the boys with its country views and fresh air. There was always something going on outside: sheep shearing, birds building nests, cattle snoozing, ants battling over a crumb of bread on the terrace. They were entertained for hours.

We were sheltered from icy winters by the huge, warm inglenook. We retreated from the steady stream of caravans, motorcycle gangs and tractors on the roads during high summer, often not seeing another soul for days on end. Home education protected us from frustration at school.

But as the boys grew and blossomed, we knew that they couldn't be held in the cwtch forever. They needed to face life and live it to the full. As they grew older we kept the house, but moved closer to the things that the boys were interested in and, ultimately, higher education.

We are going to sell the cwtch now. It has helped us, sheltered us, healed us. Now it is time for it to work its magic on another family.

If you can't have a cwtch of your own to live in, I think it's important to create one inside. Feel the sort of comfort and peace from a hug, and a sanctuary within. Whenever I have been away from Cwm Llan I try to hold a small piece of cwtch inside myself. It protects the child inside of me who is still frightened, and curious, and shy, and young.

We have travelled a lot over the years, returning to Cwm Llan like homing pigeons, older and hopefully wiser each time. Our boys will have a cwtch of their own one day. I hope when they do they will remember the halcyon days in our hug of a house, and feel very safe, and very loved.

About the Author

Marcie Layton is a memoirist, living in North Wales. She writes about Wales, her family, travel in Italy, and her experience of life on the autistic spectrum. Previously published work includes 'Fi 'di'r Deinosor', in the short story anthology *Zero Hours on the Boulevard,* published by Parthian books and her 2021 memoir *A Life Lived Behind Glass: A Journey through the Autistic Spectrum.*

Photo: Andrew Nash

Printed in Poland
by Amazon Fulfillment
Poland Sp. z o.o., Wrocław
14 July 2021

8a2022ba-483c-4e79-89c6-dd239c90ec8fR01